DATE DUE 7/19/06

AUG + 2 2006	
	WITHDRAWN
by	<

since 1983

Library of Congress Cataloging-in-Publication Data
Espeland, Pamela.
   Proud to be you : the positive identity assets / by Pamela Espeland and Elizabeth Verdick.
      p. cm. — (Adding assets series for kids)
   ISBN-13: 978-1-57542-202-2
   ISBN-10: 1-57542-202-6
  1. Self-esteem—Juvenile literature. I. Verdick, Elizabeth. II. Title. III. Series: Espeland, Pamela, Adding assets series for kids.
   BF697.5.S46E87 2006
   158.1083'4—dc22   2006016642

Search Institute® and Developmental Assets® are registered trademarks of Search Institute.

The original framework of 40 Developmental Assets (for adolescents) and the Developmental Assets for Middle Childhood were developed by Search Institute © 1997 and 2004, Minneapolis, MN 1-800-888-7828; www.search-institute.org. Used under license from Search Institute

The FACTS! (pages 8, 26, 46, and 63) are from *Coming into Their Own: How Developmental Assets Promote Positive Growth in Middle Childhood* by Peter C. Scales, Arturo Sesma Jr., and Brent Bolstrom (Minneapolis: Search Institute, 2004).

Illustrated by Chris Sharp
Cover design by Marieka Heinlen
Interior design by Crysten Puszczykowski
Index by Ina Gravitz

10 9 8 7 6 5 4 3 2 1
Printed in the United States of America

Free Spirit Publishing Inc.
217 Fifth Avenue North, Suite 200
Minneapolis, MN 55401-1299
(612) 338-2068
help4kids@freespirit.com
www.freespirit.com

Free Spirit Publishing is a member of the Green Press Initiative, and we're committed to printing our books on recycled paper containing a minimum of 30% post consumer waste (PCW). For every ton of books printed on 30% PCW recycled paper, we save 5.1 trees, 2,100 gallons of water, 114 gallons of oil, 18 pounds of air pollution, 1,230 kilowatt hours of energy, and .9 cubic yards of landfill space. At Free Spirit it's our goal to nurture not only young people, but nature too!

Printed on recycled paper
including 30%
post-consumer waste

Contents

Introduction

If you knew ways to make your life better, right now and for the future, would you try them?

We're guessing you would, and that's why we wrote this book. It's part of a series of eight books called the **Adding Assets Series for Kids.**

What Are Assets, Anyway?

When we use the word **assets**, we mean good things you need in your life and yourself.

We don't mean houses, cars, property, and jewelry—assets whose value is measured in money. We mean **Developmental Assets** that help you to be and become your best. Things like a close, loving family. A neighborhood where you feel safe. Adults you look up to and respect. And (sorry!) doing your homework.

There are 40 Developmental Assets in all. This book is about adding four of them to your life. They're called the **Positive Identity Assets.** "Positive identity" is a fancy way to say that you believe in yourself. You know that you're here on earth for a reason, even if you're not yet sure what that reason might be. You mostly feel good about yourself, even on down days. You're still a kid, but you have some say over things that happen in your life. When you imagine your future, it's exciting to think of what you might be and do someday.

The Positive Identity Assets

Asset Name	What It Means
Personal Power	You feel that you have some control over things that happen in your life.
Self-Esteem	You like yourself, and you're proud to be the person you are.
Sense of Purpose	You sometimes think about what life means and whether your life has a purpose.
Positive View of Personal Future	You feel hopeful about your own future.

Other books in the series are about the other 36 assets.* That may seem like a lot, but don't worry. You don't have to add them all at once. You don't have to add them in any particular order. But the sooner you can add them to your life, the better.

---

* If you're curious to know what the other assets are, you can read the whole list on pages 80–81.

Why You Need Assets

An organization called Search Institute surveyed hundreds of thousands of kids and teens across the United States. Their researchers found that some kids have a fairly easy time growing up, while others don't. Some kids get involved in harmful behaviors or dangerous activities, while others don't.

What makes the difference? Developmental Assets! Kids who have them are more likely to do well. Kids who don't have them are less likely to do well.

Maybe you're thinking, "Why should I have to add my own assets? I'm just a kid!" Because kids have the power to make choices in their lives. You can choose to sit back and wait for other people to help you, or you can choose to help yourself. You can also work with other people who care about you and want to help.

Many of the ideas in this book involve working with other people—like your parents, grandparents, aunts, uncles, and other family grown-ups. And your teachers, neighbors, coaches, Scout leaders, and religious leaders. They can all help add assets for you and with you.

It's likely that many of the adults in your life are already helping. In fact, an adult probably gave you this book to read.

How to Use This Book

Start by choosing **one** asset to add. Read the stories at the beginning and end of that chapter. The stories are examples of the assets in everyday life. Then pick **one** idea and try it. See how it goes. After that, try another idea, or move on to another asset.

Don't worry about being perfect or getting it right. Know that by trying, you're doing something great for yourself.

The more assets you add, the better you'll feel about yourself and your future. Soon you won't be a kid anymore. You'll be a teenager. Because you have assets, you'll feel and be a lot more sure of yourself. You'll make better decisions. You'll have a head start on success.

We wish you the very best as you add assets to your life.

Pamela Espeland and Elizabeth Verdick
Minneapolis, MN

A Few Words About Families

Kids today live in many different kinds of families.

Maybe you live with one or both of your parents. Maybe you live with other adult relatives—aunts and uncles, grandparents, grown-up brothers or sisters or cousins.

Maybe you live with a stepparent, foster parent, or guardian. Maybe you live with one of your parents and his or her life partner.

In this series, we use the word **parents** to describe the adults who care for you in your home. We also use **family adults**, **family grown-ups**, and **adults at home.** When you see any of these words, think of your own family, whatever kind it is.

Personal Power

What it means: You feel that you have some control over things that happen in your life.

Danny's Story

At recess, a big group of fifth graders heads toward the grassy field. "Kickball!" shouts a tall, athletic boy named Jake. He immediately appoints himself captain, then tells a girl named Casey that she can be second captain.

"Jake the Jock, in command," Danny mutters to his friend Amanda, who smiles.

Jake and Casey quickly start filling their teams with their favorite players and closest friends. Danny waits, the group of the unchosen growing smaller and smaller around him.

Casey picks Amanda, who drags her feet as she lines up with her teammates. Danny meets her worried eyes, knowing how much Amanda hates it when anyone feels bad. He goes cross-eyed to make her laugh.

"Why is choosing teams always such a big deal?" Danny wonders. He wishes it didn't have to be a contest, with nervous contestants shuffling their feet and staring at the ground.

6

Jake looks him over, as if Danny were a worm. "Just pick, would you?" Danny says boldly.

"Fine. I pick you," Jake says.

But when Danny goes to join the others, Jake pulls him aside and says, "Your kicking isn't terrible, but your running is lame. Remember to aim into the outfield so you've got more time to circle the bases."

Amanda overhears. "Don't pay any attention to him," she tells Danny under her breath.

"Don't worry, I won't," Danny answers. He knows he's not perfect and a lot of kids call him names like "Pudge" behind his back. All the same, he's got Amanda for a friend. As far as he's concerned, she's the prettiest, smartest girl in the school. That's one reason why he won't let the kickball scene get him down.

Even when times are tough, Danny has the *Personal Power* asset, and it gives him strength.

Think about your own life. Do you feel like you have some control or influence over things that happen to you?

If **YES**, keep reading to learn ways to make this asset even stronger.

If **NO**, keep reading to learn ways to add this asset to your life.

You can also use these ideas to help add this asset for other people—like your friends, family members, neighbors, and kids at school.

Facts!

Kids with the
Personal Power **asset:**

✔ get better grades in school and score higher on standard-ized tests

✔ are better at solving problems

✔ are less likely to use cigarettes, alcohol, and other drugs

ways to Add This Asset

 AT HOME

Look on the Bright Side. Take a quick look at the drawing on the next page. What do you see? Is the glass half empty or half full? This is a simple psychology

test that's supposed to reveal whether you're an *optimist* or a *pessimist*. Optimists are people who look on the bright side and expect good things to happen. They tend to see the glass as half full. Pessimists are people who usually expect the worst. They tend to see the glass as half empty. Experts say that being an optimist improves your mood  and your health. Why not try it? Starting now, be an optimist for the whole day (and beyond). Smile, expect the best, and do your best. Make a wish and believe it will come true.

Tip: A positive attitude is your ticket to building personal power.

Watch Your Words. Your self-talk—the things you say to yourself—can build or break your confidence. Tune in to your *inner voice,* that little voice inside your head that talks to you all day long. Does it say things like "You never do anything right," "You're so stupid," or "You're a loser"? This kind of self-talk can weaken you and steal your personal power. Guess what: You can change your inner voice. (After all, it's YOUR inner voice!) Make it say things like "I'm confident," "I have choices," and "I like myself."

> **TiP:** Imagine there's a radio playing inside your head. It's YOUR radio, so you can change the channel whenever there's a song or program that brings you down.

5 Things to Tell Yourself When Things Go Wrong

1. "It's okay if things don't go my way."

2. "I can try again."

3. "I won't let this get me down."

4. "I'll feel better about this tomorrow."

5. "I won't give up."

Build Your Skills. Being optimistic and using positive self-talk can build your personal power. But they can only take you so far. You can't build personal power without also building *skills*. What kinds of skills? All kinds. You can work on doing well in school, getting better in sports or gym, trying new activities or hobbies, reading lots of great books, strengthening your friendships, and more. The more skills you build, the more you'll be able to do, and the more personal power you'll have. Are you ready to commit? Are you ready to practice? In your journal, write *one* skill you want to build. In your planner, schedule time to start building that skill.

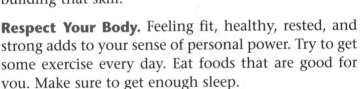

Respect Your Body. Feeling fit, healthy, rested, and strong adds to your sense of personal power. Try to get some exercise every day. Eat foods that are good for you. Make sure to get enough sleep.

Be More Responsible. If you want more control over things that happen in your life, try being more responsible. Instead of waiting for someone to tell you to clean your room, just do it. Don't put off doing your homework until someone reminds you. Volunteer for a new chore or two around the house. Keep the promises you make to family members. The more responsible you are, the more people will trust you to make good decisions—and the more decisions you'll get to make.

4 More Ways to Pump Up Your Personal Power

1. Know your worth. Not in *dollars,* of course. (You're worth way more than any amount of money in the world.) You're a completely original person, and you bring a lot to the world just because you're *you.* Never forget that.

2. Know your values. You have them, and your family has them. But maybe you all need a refresher course. Your values are the beliefs that guide your choices and behaviors. Your values help give you inner strength. Spend some time talking to your parents about how values can help strengthen you as a person and as a family.

3. Know your rights. As a human being, you have the right to think your own thoughts, form your own opinions, share your feelings, and make decisions in your life (with help from the grown-ups who care about you). When you know your rights, you can stand up for them—and that helps build your personal power.

4. Know your mission. Do you believe that you're here on earth for a purpose? That you're someone who can change the world for the better? You are, and you can! For more on this, turn to page 43 and read about the Sense of Purpose asset.

 **AT SCHOOL**

Learn as Much as You Can. Learn from your teachers and others at school. After all, that's what you're there for, isn't it? Knowledge is power! If you have problems learning, paying attention, or staying on task, talk with a teacher or your school counselor. Say that you really want to learn and ask for help.

Learn and Follow School Rules. Why risk getting in trouble for breaking a rule you don't even know about? Most schools have handbooks or handouts about the rules. Look them over. Then you can choose to follow the rules.

Solve Conflicts Peacefully. If you have a problem with someone at school, try to solve it in a peaceful way. Talk it over. Give your point of view and listen to the other person. Don't get into a fight or a shouting match. Peacefulness is power! Walk away and get help if you need it.

Make a Difference. Join a service club that works for positive change in your school, in your community, and in the world. No service club at your school? Maybe you could start one. Think of something or someone you want to help. The environment? Animals? Homeless people? Elderly people? Find friends who feel the way you do. Then find a teacher who thinks you have a good cause and is willing to sponsor your service club.

Use Your Smile Power. A great smile lights up a room. It says that you're a friendly, positive person. It makes other people want to be near you. Try smiling when you get on the bus in the morning, when you walk into a classroom, when you go into the lunchroom. See what happens.

IN YOUR NEIGHBORHOOD

★ Visit your local library. Ask the librarian to recommend books about people who overcame difficult situations in their lives. What can you learn from them?

★ Be a helper to younger kids. Spend time with them. Be someone they can look up to and learn from. Boost their personal power by showing you believe in them and want the best for them.

★ Look around your neighborhood. Do you see graffiti? Trash on the sidewalks or streets? Tell your parents or other family adults. What can you do together to make your neighborhood a better place?

 ## IN YOUR FAITH COMMUNITY

★ For many people, faith is a source of personal power. The values you learn from your faith tradition can guide you to make good decisions. So can prayer or meditation. If you belong to a faith community, talk with your religious leaders about how to strengthen your faith. Talk with your parents and other family adults about what their faith means to them.

WITH YOUR FRIENDS

★ When someone gives you a compliment, take it. If one of your friends says, "Great work!" for something you did, don't reply, "Oh, it was nothing." It was *something,* so say "Thanks!"

★ True friends help to build each other's personal power. They give each other emotional support. They have each other's backs.  They are there for each other in good times and bad. Think about your friends. Do they fit this description? The ones who do are your true friends. Try to spend more time with them.

★ If your friends take foolish risks or behave in ways you know are wrong, don't just go along. Tell them what you think and how you feel. Use your personal power and be true to yourself.

A message for you

Fears and worries can drain your personal power. While every-one feels scared and worried some of the time, no one should feel that way most or all of the time. You can learn to deal with your fears and worries. You might start by making a list. Are you scared of thunder? Spiders? The dark? Worried about your next math quiz or moving to a new neighborhood? Share your list with an adult you trust and can talk to—a parent or other family grown-up, a teacher, or a school counselor.

Visit this Web site to learn more about fears and worries (and other stuff):

www.kidshealth.org/kid

On the home page, type the word "fear" or "worry" in the search window. You'll get lists of articles written to and for kids. Click on the links to learn more.

Start Adding!

Pick at least ONE idea you've read here and give it a try. Then think about or write about what happened. Will you try other ways to build your personal power and have more control over things that happen in your life?

Back to Danny's Story

Casey's team is up first, and they manage to score eight runs while taking up half of recess time. Danny can tell that Jake is anxious for his team to get time to play—and win.

Finally, Jake's team is up. The bases are quickly filled, and soon the runners will start coming home. Jake looks pumped up, and he checks his watch before telling the team, "Not much time left, so let's pull together and win this thing! The score is eight to zip."

Two outs and six runs later, Danny is still waiting for his turn. Jake had put him at the very end of the line, probably hoping that Danny would never get a chance to be up. Danny watches as two girls ahead of him each take their turns. One makes it to third base, the other to second. Danny finally reaches the front of the line.

"Casey's team is only two runs ahead," Jake says to Danny. "Don't mess this up. All you need to do is bring the two runners home. Stop at first base and let someone else take it from there."

"Right," Danny replies, waiting for the kickball to roll toward him. He kicks with all his strength, feeling the ball connect with his foot. "Yes!" he exclaims as the ball soars. He heads toward first and reaches it.

The ball bounces once and Amanda catches it. Danny takes a chance and runs toward second base. The other two runners reach home, and Danny quickly gauges where Amanda is—still far enough away, he realizes. He chugs toward third, even though Jake yells, "Stay! Stay!"

Rounding third, Danny looks for Amanda again. "Where is she?" he wonders. Suddenly, he sees her sprawled on the field, where she probably tripped on her own large feet.

"Home! Home!" Jake and his teammates yell. They motion Danny forward.

"Get up, Amanda!" Casey shouts.

But Amanda is hurt. She's holding her ankle, and Danny decides he's more concerned about her than the game. Halfway to home, he raises his hands for a timeout.

When he reaches Amanda, she looks at him and says, "You should have kept going. You just blew your chance for kickball fame!"

"All thanks to you, Bigfoot," Danny says with a grin. He carefully helps Amanda stand up.

The recess monitor blows the whistle, signaling that it's time to head back in. Casey, Jake, and the rest of the players surround Amanda and Danny.

"Tie game, then," Danny says.

"Could have been a win," Jake replies gruffly, picking up the kickball.

Amanda looks at Danny with a worried look on her face. *"Amanda,"* Danny reassures her, "you should know by now that I don't care what Jake says. It was my choice to call that timeout, and I'm glad I did."

"Rock on, Danny," says Casey. "You're the best sport I know. Here, let me help you get Amanda to the nurse." She smiles at Danny warmly, and together he, Casey, and a limping Amanda make their way off the field.

Self-Esteem

Lisa's Story

"Aargh!" Lisa exclaims, plunking herself on the couch next to her dad.

"Whoa," he says. "What's up with you?"

"I just had an Alexander day," she replies. "Terrible, horrible, no good, and very bad!" Lisa is referring to a children's book she and her dad used to read together.

"Uh-oh. Want to talk about it?"

Lisa tells him everything that went wrong. First, she got soaked at the bus stop. Then a boy at school called her hair "stringy." Lunch was icky overcooked fish sticks. During math, she messed up her long division problem on the board. She forgot to bring home her backpack.

"And on top of it all," she says, "I feel like a freak because the rubber bands on my new braces keep snapping off when I'm eating or laughing!"

"Wow," her dad says, putting his arms around her. "That's an Alexander day for sure."

Lisa snuggles into him and breathes in the scent of his wool sweater. Their fluffy little dog, Barney, jumps up on the couch and plops himself in Lisa's lap.

"Barney agrees," she says, pulling the dog close.

"Well, maybe your day is about to get better. I'm making tacos for dinner."

Lisa perks up. "Really?"

"Yep, and Mom's bringing home dessert. I think she had a bad day, too," her dad replies.

Lisa gives a little laugh, knowing how her mom is always saying that chocolate can cure anything.

"Dad?" Lisa asks. "Is my hair stringy? And do I look like a loser with these braces?"

"No, and no. I think you're beautiful inside and out."

"You always say that mushy stuff," Lisa replies. But inside, she feels better.

Her dad hugs her and asks if she wants to help with dinner.

"Actually, I'm just going to write in my journal for a while, if you don't mind," she says.

"I don't mind at all," he replies as he gets up from the couch. He stretches, pats Barney on the head, and heads for the kitchen.

Lisa is working on the *Self-Esteem* asset.

Think about your own life. Do you like (or love) yourself? Do you feel proud of the things you do, and more importantly, proud of who you are?

If **YES**, keep reading to learn ways to make this asset even stronger.

If **NO**, keep reading to learn ways to add this asset to your life.

You can also use these ideas to help add this asset for other people—like your friends, family members, neighbors, and kids at school.

> ## Facts!
>
> **Kids with the *Self-Esteem* asset:**
>
> ✔ **care more about school**
>
> ✔ **have fewer behavior problems**
>
> ✔ **take better care of their bodies**

ways to Add This Asset

 **AT HOME**

Don't Bash Yourself. Do you ever compare yourself to other people and end up feeling bad? Maybe you admire your sister's talent on the playing field, your brother's successes in school, or a friend's expensive clothes, and you think you're a big loser. Self-bashing doesn't get you anywhere but down. Avoid comparing yourself to others in a negative way. Remember, you're *you,* and that's not a bad thing. See "Watch Your Words" on pages 9–10 and "4 More Ways to Pump Up Your Personal Power" on pages 12–13.

Boost Each Other Up. Talk to the grown-ups at home about what makes them feel proud of you. (It's okay to ask this, by the way. It's not like you're fishing for compliments.) *Example:* You could simply ask, "Dad, are there some things I do that make you proud of me?" Return the favor by telling that person what makes you proud of him or her. And don't forget your siblings. Notice their achievements and say, "Way to go!" Or write things you like about them on sticky notes and post them where they'll see them (on a headboard, in a notebook, on a bathroom mirror).

> **TiP:** Make it a habit in your family to boost each other up. You'll all feel stronger and closer.

Keep Journals About Your Life. Some of the world's most famous people kept journals about their lives. They wrote about their thoughts, feelings, great ideas, and impressions of the world. Why? Did they know they would someday be famous, and that other people

would want to learn more about their childhoods and private thoughts? Some may have. But many simply believed in themselves and were curious about their own inner workings. They explored and saved their personal thoughts by writing them down, and you can do that, too. By writing or drawing in your journal, you'll get to know yourself better. That kind of "self-awareness" helps you appreciate yourself more. And the great thing is, you can go back and look at your journals later on and think, "Wow, I can't believe that happened to me!" or "That was an awesome day! I'm glad I wrote it all down."

Follow One Journaling Rule. You can journal in a blank book, in a notebook, in a sketchbook, or on a computer—whatever suits your style. There's just one rule you need to follow: **Date Every Entry!** In other words, include the date every time you write. That way, you can track how your thoughts and feelings, attitudes and goals change over the years.

> **TIP:** Some people keep journals they don't mind others reading. You can keep yours top-secret if you want.

Journaling Ideas to Try

Use these "prompts" to help you get started.
Or come up with your own ideas. Remember:
Your journal is all about *you*, which means
you can write anything you want.

★ Who am I?

★ What's unique about me?

★ What makes me laugh?

★ What do I care about the most?

★ What makes me happy?

★ What makes me feel crazy?

★ What do I wish for?

★ Who loves me?

★ What's my biggest dream?

★ If I could go anywhere, where would I go?

★ What are my talents or strengths?

★ What made me laugh today?

★ What am I grateful for?

★ Who are my role models and why?

★ What did I see today that surprised me?

★ What makes me *me*?

Celebrate Your Cultural Identity. Talk to the adults at home about your cultural roots. Where do you come from? Who were your ancestors? Learn your culture's stories and traditions. Be proud of who you are.

Make a Proud-of-Me List. In your journal or on a separate sheet of paper, write the things you do that make you feel good about yourself and proud of yourself. *Examples:* "I'm a good speller." "I know a lot about birds." "I helped my big sister when the computer crashed." "People know they can count on me." "I made dinner for my family on Thursday—and they ate it!" During times when you're feeling not-so-good about yourself, look at your list.

Have a Purpose for Your Life. Know that you're here for a reason. See pages 43–59 for more on this topic.

Self-Esteem Don'ts and Do's

DON'T compare yourself to other people in a negative way.	**DO** know that you're one of a kind—a unique individual with your own unique abilities. There's no one else on earth exactly like you.
DON'T think that you have to please everyone.	**DO** work to please yourself.
DON'T set impossible goals for yourself.	**DO** set goals you can reasonably reach—and goals you have to *s-t-r-e-t-c-h* to reach.
DON'T try to be perfect.	**DO** try for your personal best in the things you really care about.

Take Care of Your Body. Exercise, eat right, get enough sleep, and use good hygiene. (You know—brush your teeth, wash your hair, take showers, clean and trim your fingernails . . . and don't forget your toenails either.) See pages 32–33.

7 Ways to Clean Up Your Act

Want to know a simple way to raise your self-esteem? Keep yourself neat and clean. Here's how.

1. Wash your hands—lots!
Do it before you eat, after you eat, after you play outside, after going to the bathroom, and after petting your pets. Wash for at least 30 seconds, which is about the time it takes to sing "Happy Birthday" two times.

2. Bathe or shower more often. Try to bathe at night or take a quick shower in the morning—whatever you prefer. If you don't have time to shower before school, be sure to at least wash your face.

3. Use deodorant if you need it. If you're ready to start using deodorant or antiperspirant, talk to your dad or mom about what to buy. Don't be embarrassed— sweaty pits are normal.

4. Carry mints. You just ate garlicky pizza for lunch, and you don't have time to brush your teeth before your next class. You'll be breathing all over your friends and classmates, so why not pop a breath mint? You can keep some in your pocket or backpack— and share them with anyone else who ate the pizza, too.

5. Don't forget to floss. Flossing your teeth is part of a healthy daily dental routine. You can ask a family grown-up or your dentist to show you how to do it.

6. Bring a comb or brush. For quick touchups during the day, keep a comb or brush in your locker or backpack.

7. Lip balm to the rescue. Got dry, chapped, sore lips? Carry some lip balm in your pocket. Your lips will thank you.

A message for you

Some kids (and adults) are confused about what self-esteem really means. It doesn't mean thinking about yourself all the time. It doesn't mean bragging about yourself, showing off, or being stuck-up. It doesn't mean putting other people down because you think you're better than they are. It's not about flattery and empty praise.

Self-esteem means feeling strong and secure inside yourself. It means feeling good about your values and beliefs, your skills and abilities, how you treat others, and the good things you do. Also, it's not possible to have "too much self-esteem." In fact, the more you have, the better!

Here are four reasons why you need self-esteem:

1. Self-esteem gives you the courage to take positive risks. You know that if you fail, it's not the end of the world.

2. Self-esteem gives you the strength to resist negative risks and peer pressure. You respect yourself too much to do something dumb.

3. Self-esteem makes you strong. You can cope with whatever life throws your way.

4. Self-esteem makes you *resilient*. That means you can bounce back from problems, mistakes, disappointments, and failures.

AT SCHOOL

★ School is a place where a lot of kids bash themselves. Someone else is always more popular, more successful, better-looking, smarter, or cooler. Don't compare yourself to others—and don't beat yourself up for not being like them. Tune into your inner voice. Keep your self-talk positive.

★ Avoid cliques. Nothing can make you feel sicker quicker. Cliques love shutting people out, putting people down, and acting like they're better than everyone else. Who needs them? Find friends who are accepting and supportive.

★ If someone is bullying you, tell a teacher. Being bullied is bad for your self-esteem. It's hard to feel good about yourself when you're being picked on or threatened.

> **TIP:** If someone else is being bullied, speak up for the person or get help from a grown-up. When you know something is wrong and you do something about it, you help others *and* yourself.

★ Building relationships builds your self-esteem. When you connect with others, you feel better about yourself. Take the first step toward making a new friend at school. Say hi in the hallway, hang out on the playground, or invite the person to sit with you at lunch.

IN YOUR NEIGHBORHOOD

★ Treat younger kids with respect. Notice them, spend time with them, and tell them what you like about them. Often, older kids act like younger kids are invisible. Maybe you've been there and you know how it feels.

★ Helping others is a great way to build your self-esteem. It's natural to feel good about yourself when you put a smile on someone else's face. Talk with your parents or other family adults. Is there a neighbor who could use your help? Maybe you could shovel a sidewalk, mow a lawn, or paint a fence.

IN YOUR FAITH COMMUNITY

★ Did you know that belonging to a faith community can build your self-esteem? Studies have shown that kids who participate in religious activities feel better about themselves than kids who don't. If you're not part of a faith community and you think you might want to be, talk with your parents or other family grown-ups. Maybe you can go to services or meetings with another relative or a family friend.

★ Celebrating birthdays is a simple way to boost kids' self-esteem. Maybe you could sing "Happy Birthday" in religion class. Maybe the names of kids with birthdays could be listed in the bulletin, or even mentioned in the sermon or homily. Ask your religion teacher.

WITH YOUR FRIENDS

★ A friend says something nice to you and you feel happy. Or a friend says something mean to you and you feel sad. Remember those feelings when deciding how to treat your friends. Build each other up instead of tearing each other down. Give each other verbal high-fives. *Examples:* "I like your smile." "Thanks for listening the other day." "Congratulations on finishing the race." "I love your poem." "You're so creative!"

★ Sometime when you and your friends get together, bring copies of the kids' and teens' magazines you like to read. Take a look at the articles and ads. What are they trying to tell you or sell you? That to feel good about yourself, you have to look a certain way or drink a certain type of soda? Talk about this as a group. You might decide not to believe the hype.

A special message for girls

Researchers have found that girls' self-esteem peaks when they are 9 years old and starts falling after that. The older girls get, the less confident they feel about themselves. Mostly, they are unhappy with the way they look. Many girls start dieting at the age of 10 because they want to be like the super-thin models in magazines and on TV. Low self-esteem puts girls at risk for being depressed and having eating disorders. They are more likely to start using alcohol and other drugs.

If you're a girl, what do you need? Adults you can trust and talk to. Positive role models. Self-respect. Goals you really care about. Meaningful things to do. Opportunities to build your skills and strengths. Friends who will support you. And fewer fashion magazines!

If you're starting to think you're not good enough, pretty enough, or perfect enough (or if you've thought that for a while), find someone to talk to—a friend who understands, a family adult who will listen, a teacher or coach or school counselor.

Start Adding!

Pick at least ONE idea you've read here and give it a try. Then think about or write about what happened. Will you try another way to build your self-esteem?

Back to Lisa's Story Lisa leans back into the couch cushions, her journal resting on her knees. Barney curls into a ball at her feet. She reads a few of her older journal entries—things she titled "Stuff I'm Grateful For" and "Things That Make Me Laugh."

Soon she's smiling as she remembers the good times: taking walks in the fall, playing softball with her friends, hanging out with her mom while she put photos in the family scrapbooks. Lisa laughs out loud while reading funny entries about her teacher's corny jokes and how Barney loves to steal Dad's dirty socks and hide them in his dog bed.

"I guess my life's not so bad," she thinks. She turns to a fresh page in her journal and tries to put her mixed-up feelings into words.

Today wasn't the greatest (smelly cafeteria fish sticks, cold rain on my head, homework undone 'cause I left it in my locker). Sometimes, I worry that I look like a dork. Whenever I smile now, all I see is metal. But I'm still ME. Mom and Dad say that's a great thing to be.

P.S. I'm lucky I was born in this family!

P.P.S. I HAVE THE BEST DOG IN THE WORLD!!

Lisa slams her journal shut and stands up. "Dad!" she shouts. "This bad day is over—I'm coming to help you cook now!"

She heads for the kitchen with Barney at her heels.

Sense of Purpose

What it means: You sometimes think about what life means and whether your life has a purpose.

Art's Story

Art leaves his sixth-grade classroom feeling weak in the knees. He's just received his first-ever failing grade—in science! Science has always been his best subject. But somehow he's scored poorly on the last three tests, and it has hurt his confidence.

He kicks his locker door shut with a bang. "It's not like I'll ever be Mr. Popularity or a star athlete," he thinks. "And no girls ever even *talk* to me." He slings his backpack over his shoulder, clutching his test in one hand. "But at least I was always a good science geek." The "was" worries him.

Outdoors, where the buses wait, a gust of wind blows Art's curly red hair. He pushes his glasses up on his nose. The clouds darken. Suddenly, fat drops of rain splash the ground and Art quickly climbs the bus stairs and finds a seat.

He doesn't really mind the rain right now—it suits his dark mood. "Aside from Scouts, all I've got is science. It's who I *am*," he tells himself. He folds his test and shoves it in his jeans pocket.

The wind shakes the bus. Some of the kids laugh nervously while others yell, "Check it out!" Art watches the wind bend the tree branches at odd angles, surprised at the intensity of this spring storm.

The students who get off the bus put their backpacks and books over their heads to shield themselves from the rain. Art grabs a cap from the bottom of his

own pack and puts in on, thinking about how his Scouting experience has taught him to be prepared. "At least I did *one* thing right today," he mutters.

At last, the bus reaches his stop. And just as suddenly as it started, the storm dies down. Art climbs from the bus and heads toward his small house. He sees him mom in the doorway, and his heart sinks.

She waves, opens the door, and says, "Lucky you! You just missed getting soaked."

"Not so lucky," he says miserably. He fishes in his pocket and pulls out his wrinkled test. Hot tears sting his eyes.

"Oh no," his mom says, looking at his test and the big red F at the top. "Art, you studied so hard!"

"I know. Mom, I can't talk about it now. I'll be back in a little while, okay?" He turns and heads toward a patch of woods at the end of the block, one of his favorite places in the world.

Art's *Sense of Purpose* has been shaken.

Think about your own life. Do you ever wonder if you were born for a reason? Do you think about whether you have a special purpose here on planet Earth? Do you wonder about the meaning of life?

If **YES**, keep reading to learn ways to make this asset even stronger.

If **NO**, keep reading to learn ways to add this asset to your life.

Facts!

Kids with the *Sense of Purpose* asset:

✔ are less likely to do risky or dangerous things

✔ are less *aggressive* (pushy and violent)

✔ feel that they have more control over their lives

You can also use these ideas to help add this asset for other people—like your friends, family members, neighbors, and kids at school.

ways to Add This Asset

 **AT HOME**

Write About Your Life Purpose. This isn't anything you'll be graded on, so don't worry about perfect grammar and punctuation. Instead, just take the time to write your answers to some of the big questions: *Who am I? Why was I born? Why am I here? What is my purpose in life?* Have you ever thought about these things? Maybe you wonder about these questions for a moment now and then, but here's your chance to do some heavy thinking about them. What do you hope to accomplish now while you're young, and later when you're grown up? Do you have dreams of changing the world, and if so, how?

> **TiP:** Your life purpose doesn't have to be a someday-when-I'm-older thing. It can also be a right-now thing. What's a good reason to wake up in the morning? Maybe that's your life purpose at this point in time.

A message for you

If you sometimes or often have thoughts like, "I'm no good," "I should never have been born," or "What's the point, anyway?" you're dealing with feelings that are too tough to handle on your own. Please seek out an adult you trust and talk about what you're going through. You can go to a parent, teacher, religious leader, school counselor, or someone else who will listen. Here's why: You might have deep-down feelings of sadness or pain, and you need some help dealing with them. You *can* feel better. Don't wait any longer to get help.

Discover Your Passions. "Passion" sounds like a weird word, doesn't it? We're not talking about the kissing kind of passion—we're talking about a feeling of inspiration and excitement that makes you want to get up and do whatever it is you love to do. What's *your* passion? Science, math, reading, drawing comic strips, volunteering, playing drums, learning a new language, collecting, dancing, skateboarding? Whatever it is, find a way to do it or do *more* of it. You'll build your sense of purpose and get more excited about life's possibilities.

> **Tip:** Ask family members what their passions are. Maybe you share a passion with your mom or dad, a cousin, an uncle, or a grandparent.

Make a Passion Plan. Pick one of your passions, then decide what you'd like to do with it someday. *Examples:* "I love to read books—maybe someday I'll write them." "I love to run! Maybe someday I'll run a marathon . . . or compete in the Olympics!" "I love to draw pictures of buildings and houses. I'd like to be an architect someday." Guess what? You've just set a goal for yourself. Now, how will you go for it? What's a good first step to take?

Talk About Big Stuff. What do you and your family usually talk about? If you're like many families, you probably talk about anything from how your day went to which brand of toothpaste you like best or who forgot to change the toilet paper roll. That's all part of family life, but don't forget that home is a place to have bigger conversations, too. Talk with the adults in your family about their sense of purpose. What do they believe about their own life purpose and yours? What are their thoughts on how the universe was created? What are their dreams for humankind?

Respect the Earth and All Who Live Here. Our world is an amazing place—so much bigger than the view you see outside your door each day. Do you ever stop to think about just how HUGE this planet is and how many different types of people live here? And how many different kinds of animals, reptiles, bugs, trees, and plants there are? Go take a look at a globe today, either at home, school, or the library. Research some of your favorite plants or animals. Appreciate just how much life there is out there—and how much there is to live for.

Think About How You Spend Your Time. Maybe you're super-busy . . . but busy doing what? Try cutting down on your TV, telephone, and computer time. Spend more time reading, daydreaming, studying, helping out, doing hobbies, or following your passions.

Keep a Scrapbook. Collect stories and articles about people who do good things in the world. Save them in a scrapbook. Add your own notes about why you find them inspiring.

Dr. Martin Luther King Jr.

AT SCHOOL

★ See if you can start a People with Purpose bulletin board in your classroom. Bring in pictures and stories of people who have done great things. You might ask your school's media specialist to point you toward books or articles.

Two People with Purpose

★ Nine-year-old Michael Fox was walking home from school one day when he looked through a fence at the backyard of a veterinary clinic. What he saw changed his life. There was a big trash bin full of dead dogs and cats. He never found out why they were there, but he decided right then that he would spend his life helping animals. Today Michael Fox is a famous veterinarian, animal activist, and author. He has written more than 40 books and thousands of articles. You might visit the library and look for some of his books or read his newspaper column, "Animal Doctor." Can't find it in the paper? Ask an adult to help you find it on the United Feature Syndicate Web site: *www.unitedfeatures.com.*

continued

★ Ann Belles was nine years old when she saw the movie *Oliver*, based on Charles Dickens' novel about orphan boys. She knew then that someday she would adopt orphan children. She started out as a foster parent at age 19. So far, Ann and her husband, Jim Silcock, have adopted 31 boys from all over the world. Most were considered "unadoptable" because of their age, behavior problems, disabilities, or other reasons. You can read about Ann and Jim's family at this Web site: *www.allourboys.com.*

P.S. What do Michael and Ann have in common? You're right—they were both nine years old when they discovered their life's purpose. So don't let anyone tell you that you're too young to have a sense of purpose.

★ Try to find purpose in what you're learning in school. Maybe you think that math is useless or reading stories is a big waste of time. And unless you plan to teach history someday, why bother learning about it, right? In fact, it takes all kinds of skills to make a living—and all kinds of learning to have an interesting life. If you really can't understand why you have to study some things, talk with your teacher.

 IN YOUR NEIGHBORHOOD

★ Interview neighbors to learn their sense of purpose. You might ask questions like these: "What do you like to do?" "How long have you been excited about it?" "When did you first discover that you like it? How old were you?" "What do you like about it most?" "What advice do you have for people who haven't yet discovered what they like to do?"

> **TiP:** Interview kids and teens as well as grown-ups. Remember Michael Fox and Ann Belles were nine years old when they found their life purpose.

IN YOUR FAITH COMMUNITY

★ Interview members of your faith community to learn their sense of purpose. Maybe everyone in your religion class could interview one person, then you could share what you learn.

★ For many people, faith is what gives them a sense of purpose in life. They know they're here for a reason because their faith tells them so. Other people discover their sense of purpose by getting involved in their faith community. Many famous singers (like Aretha Franklin and Al Green) found their gift for music in the gospel choir at their church. What does your faith tradition say about meaning and purpose?

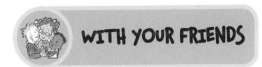

WITH YOUR FRIENDS

★ Here's a conversation-starter for a slumber party or just-hanging-out-time: "If you could do only ONE thing with your life, what would it be?" Try to take the question seriously (while still having fun). Who knows, someone might discover his or her life purpose!

★ Talk about other big questions with your friends. Why were you born? Why are you here? What's the point? What are your hopes and dreams? What do you want to be remembered for someday?

Start Adding!

Pick at least ONE idea you've read here and give it a try. Then think about or write about what happened. Will you try another idea to find—or follow—your life purpose?

Back to Art's Story

The air smells fresh and wet; mud squelches beneath Art's feet. Surveying the storm damage, he notices fallen branches and flowers drooping on heavy stems. In the woods, he leans against a damp tree trunk and absentmindedly kicks his heel against the bark.

Art can't believe he's so down about a test. He tries to reassure himself by thinking of his favorite inventor, Thomas Edison. His teachers thought he was hopeless, and he nearly failed school.

Out of the corner of his eye, Art sees something move low to the ground. He turns and looks, and then catches his breath when he realizes a tiny bird is hobbling in the wet grass. Art instinctively looks for clues—he notices the bird's bit of downy feathering, small tail, and open eyes, all of which tell him it's a nestling. In other words, it's not a young bird learning to fly but a baby that will die if left on its own.

"You belong back in your nest," Art says softly. He decides it's up to him to save the bird—but how?

Just then, he sees his mom picking her way through brambles and fallen branches. "There you are," she says, and Art motions for her to approach quietly. He points to the fragile bird, and his mom looks at it with a mix of surprise and concern.

"Its nest must be right around here," she whispers.

"I think that's it up there," Art replies, pointing toward a low tree branch above his head. "The storm probably blew the little guy out of his nest. But he doesn't look injured."

"Poor thing." His mom peers up into the tree. "So, what do you think we should do, Art?"

"Mom, I bet I can climb up there. It's not that high, and you know I've been climbing these trees since I was little."

She smiles and rolls her eyes. "You always *have* been determined, that's for sure."

Art gives her a grin, forgetting all about the test and his worries about being a hopeless case. "If you get me a shoebox, I can put the bird in it and climb up. I know I can do it, Mom. He's depending on us."

His mom agrees to the plan and goes off in search of a box. She returns a little while later and hands him the box that held his new gym shoes. Art notices the expression on her face.

"What's that look you're giving me, Mom?" he asks.

"Well," she says, drawing out the word, "*this* is science." She peers at him expectantly, waiting for him to understand.

"Ah, Mom, it's just me helping a wet bird get back home," he says, scooping the nestling gently into the box.

"It's more than that," she insists.

Art looks down at the wobbly bird with its over-sized feet, wide beak, and bumpy patches of skin. "Okay, I get it now, Mom," he says. Then he adds, "Everything's going to be okay." He's not sure if he's talking to the bird, his mom, or himself. As he starts to climb the tree, he feels as if there's nothing he can't do.

Positive View of Personal Future

What it means: You feel hopeful about your own future.

Janelle's Story

"Mom, *please* don't look at me that way," Janelle says while rubbing sunscreen on her arms.

"Well, I can't say I'm not disappointed. Dance team is a big part of your life. We all know how much you love it."

"Yeah, well, diabetes is a big part of my life too. Unfortunately." She smears sunscreen on her face and puts on her in-line skates. "I'll be on the path, Mom. Later." Janelle avoids her mother's gaze but somehow can feel it as she skates down the driveway.

The sun warms her face, and Janelle skates hard to try to forget her worries. "What if I'm making a mistake not going out for the team again?" she wonders, then pushes the thought from her mind.

In many ways, Janelle is glad that everyone trusts her to take care of herself: her mom, her stepdad, her doctor. She's grateful that they let her get an insulin pump, which makes it possible to live a more normal

life. Instead of having to test her blood and get insulin shots, she wears the pump all the time. Of course, she's happier about that. And yet . . . Janelle has to admit she feels—what? Sad? Let down? Or maybe like she's letting *others* down?

After skating a while, Janelle heads home for a drink of water. As she enters the kitchen, her stepbrother, Ian, walks up to her and demands, "What's this I hear about you quitting the Diamonds?" He crosses his arms and looks at her seriously.

"Stop trying to be my parent," Janelle says, reaching into the cupboard for a glass. "You're two years younger than me, you know."

Ignoring her, Ian presses on, saying, "You've been on the team a long time now, and you're one of the best dancers, and you know it!"

Janelle takes a gulp, sets down her glass, and points to her pump. It looks like a small pager worn on her waistband. A clear tube runs from the pump to her abdomen, where it's attached to her body by a small needle. "*This* changes everything," she says.

"Why?" Ian asks simply.

"It's a girl thing, you wouldn't understand," she says, looking away.

"I would too," Ian answers.

"No you wouldn't!" she cries. "No one does!" She runs to her room and shuts the door behind her.

> The *Positive View of Personal Future* asset could change Janelle's outlook.

Think about your own life. Do you feel excited about the future? Do you have big dreams for yourself? Do you look forward to each new day?

If **YES**, keep reading to learn ways to make this asset even stronger.

If **NO**, keep reading to learn ways to add this asset to your life.

You can also use these ideas to help add this asset for other people—like your friends, family members, neighbors, and kids at school.

Facts!

Kids with the *Positive View of Personal Future* asset:

✔ are better readers

✔ feel less anxious and more secure

✔ get along better with their friends

ways to Add This Asset

At Home

Write Your Story. Pretend you're a reporter interviewing your future self. Who might that person be? A poet? A politician? A detective? A circus performer?

Your future self can be anything you want. Ask yourself questions like "How did you choose this career?" and "What's the secret of your success?" Then write your story as if you were putting it together for a magazine. You can type it up on a computer, if you have access to one. You can even add pictures of yourself dressed the way you might look 10 or 15 years from now. (Draw the pictures or have someone take photos of you in costume.)

Try to Be Optimistic. If you haven't read "Look on the Bright Side" on pages 8–9, take a moment and read it now. Another word for optimism is *hopefulness*. Are you a hopeful person? Do you expect that things will generally turn out well? Are you excited about the future?

Pay Attention to Your Self-Talk. Go back to the "Personal Power" chapter again and read (or re-read) "Watch Your Words" on pages 9–10. It matters what you say to yourself about yourself. In fact, your opinion is the one that matters most. Other people can think well of you, but if you don't, you won't feel good about yourself—or your future.

Plan for Your Future. Talk to the grown-ups in your family about what the future holds for you. If you dream of being a pilot or a book illustrator, for example, how do you go about making that a reality? What steps do you need to take to set out on the right path? What kind of schooling will you need after high school? How will you know what direction to go, and who will help you determine what you need to succeed? You're young, and you've got lots of time to figure it all out . . . but it doesn't hurt to think about what you'll need for future success.

Learn What Others Have Done. For most people, success doesn't land in their laps—it takes big dreams, hard work, and plenty of guts. Need proof? Read some biographies and autobiographies of famous people. You'll learn about all the mistakes they made and hurdles they overcame. Talk about inspiring!

Check It Out

While planning for your future, it might be fun to sit down at the computer with a family adult and visit these Web sites.

What Do You Like?
www.bls.gov/k12/
Find out about all kinds of jobs—what they're like, how to get ready, how much they pay, and more—from the Bureau of Labor Statistics.

Career Voyages
www.careervoyages.gov/students-main.cfm
Learn about different types of careers, find out the knowledge and skills you need, and get information about education and training opportunities. The Web site is a collaboration between the U.S. Department of Labor and the U.S. Department of Education.

Find a whole list of career-related Web sites for kids here:
www.kids.gov/k_careers.htm

Have fun exploring!

Describe Your Future Self. Write one sentence that describes the person you want to be someday. You can write it in your journal or on a scrap of paper to keep in your wallet, backpack, or planner. Look at your sentence every month or so. Change it if you need to or want to.

Collect Quotes That Make You Smile (or Think). Libraries have lots of quotations books. You can also find Web sites with collections of quotes by well-known people. When you're reading magazines or news items, copy down any quotes that really move you, whether they're the words of celebrities, newsmakers, or regular kids. You can store them in your journal or planner, or put the ones you love most on a bulletin board where you can read them at a glance. *Example:* "If you think you can do a thing or think you can't do a thing, you're right." This quote is by Henry Ford, the man who made automotive history. His words were clever, but they also spoke to the power of *positive thinking.* If you put your mind to something and believe in your heart that you can do it, your chances of success go *way* up.

More Quotes for Your Collection

"Follow your bliss."
—Joseph Campbell*

"If you can dream it, you can do it."
—Walt Disney

"Dream the biggest dream for yourself. Hold the highest vision of life for yourself."
—Duke Ellington

"The future belongs to those who believe in the beauty of their dreams."
—Eleanor Roosevelt

---

* Your *bliss* is whatever makes you really, *really* happy.

Grow Your Funny Bone. "Laughter is the best medicine," or so the saying goes. In fact, experts have found that having a sense of humor, laughing, and smiling can keep you not only happier but healthier, too. That's because laughter releases feel-good chemicals in your body and gives you a sunnier outlook on life. You can grow your funny bone in lots of ways. *Examples:* Learn jokes and riddles, be silly with your brothers and sisters, watch comedians on TV, rent funny movies.

X-treme Example: Pick your funniest friend and write your own comedy routine together. Perform it in front of each other, and once you've had enough practice, do your stand-up routine for family and friends. If you can borrow or rent a video camera, tape your performance so you can watch it whenever you need a laugh.

Keep Adding Assets to Your Life. Maybe the Positive Identity assets are the first ones you're learning about. Or maybe you've read other books in the Adding Assets Series for Kids and are working on things like Positive Peer Influence, Caring, Creative Activities, and Resistance Skills. Remember that the more assets you have, the more likely you are to do well in life—and the brighter your future will be.

A message for you

Maybe you have a health condition, a disability, or a family issue that sets you apart in some way and makes your life more of a challenge. If so, it may not always be easy to look on the bright side or see the future in a positive light—all the *more* reason to do things that help you feel proud of who you are and what you can accomplish. Who can you talk to when times are tough or when you're worried about your future? Your dad or mom? Your doctor or counselor? A religious leader or mentor? Have you thought about joining a support group for kids who have issues similar to yours? You may find it helpful to talk to people your age who've been there and really understand what you're facing.

 AT SCHOOL

★ Be serious about school and learning. If you find this hard to do, and if school seems like a big waste of time, talk with your teachers. Say that you really *want* to do well in school, but you're feeling stuck or not sure where to start. Ask for their help.

★ Try to look forward to each new school day. Start the day by thinking of *one* thing you're excited about. ***Examples:*** Sitting with your friends at lunch. Completing a tough math quiz. Band practice. Being the after-school crossing guard. What else?

★ Get involved in a service club or volunteer activity. When you help other people, you tend to feel more hopeful about the future—because you already know you can make a difference. You're doing it right now!

IN YOUR NEIGHBORHOOD

★ Talk with neighbors you admire. Ask them about their childhood years and how they got where they are today. Do they have any advice to share with you?

★ Help younger kids look forward to the future. Tell them about fun things you're doing in school, in Scouts, and in other groups you belong to. Show by example that growing up is exciting, not scary. Maybe they think they'll never be able to read big books, or work hard math problems, or hit a softball as far as you can. Build their confidence. Say they'll get better at all kinds of things as they get older—just like you.

IN YOUR FAITH COMMUNITY

★ The word *faith* means belief, confidence, trust, and hope. When you have faith, you look forward to the future, because you believe and trust that things will work out. You might talk with your religion class about how your faith affects your view of the future.

★ Identify positive, successful adults in your faith community. See if some of them can visit your religion class to talk about their lives, answer questions, and offer advice. You might also see if older teens in your faith community can come to your class.

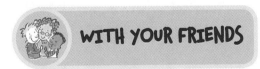

WITH YOUR FRIENDS

★ Share your dreams with each other. Support and encourage each other to make your dreams come true.

★ Talk about what the future might bring—and what you hope it will bring. You might ask each other questions like these: "What do you want to be when you grow up? Why?" "Where do you want to live?" "Do you think you'll get married someday? Will you have children?" "How will you change the world?" "What is your biggest hope for the future?" "Do you think we'll still be friends ten years from now? Twenty? What about when we're really old?"

Start Adding!

Pick at least ONE idea you've read here and give it a try. Then think about or write about what happened. Will you try another way to be hopeful about your future?

Back to Janelle's Story

"Knock, knock." Janelle's mom says, while tapping softly on the bedroom door. "Phone. It's Marcie."

Like Janelle, Marcie has been on the Diamonds team for several years, and Janelle considers her one of her best friends.

"Hi, Marcie," says Janelle.

Without even saying hi, Marcie blurts out, "You can't quit! We *need* you."

"How'd you know I was leaving the team?" Janelle asks.

"Ian called me."

"He what?" Janelle says in surprise. "Listen, Marcie, I don't want to wear a pump when I'm dancing in a leotard. The competition judges won't know what it is. I'll feel too self-conscious."

"That's not a good reason, Janelle. Look at *me*—I'm like two feet taller than everyone on the team. Don't you think I get self-conscious?"

After talking for a while longer, Janelle agrees to rethink her decision. Right after she hangs up, the phone rings again. It's Sierra and Danielle, two more Diamonds. Turns out Ian had called them, too.

"Team tryouts are at the end of the week, and you better be there," they warn. "We'll drag you to the studio ourselves if we have to."

Janelle imagines them yanking her down the street, and she has to laugh. But still, her heart is filled with doubt.

Soon after, another teammate calls, and then another and another. They say things like, "Janelle, who cares about a pump? It's no big deal." Each of the Diamonds tells Janelle that she'd miss her if she were to quit. Tina even says, "*You're* the one who always keeps *us* going. That's why it's so weird to be convincing you!"

After all the calls, Janelle plops down on her bed to think. She realizes she never knew how much the team cared about her—or how much Ian did, for that matter. She knows it must have taken courage for an eleven-year-old boy to call up a bunch of thirteen-year-old girls he barely knows.

Janelle gets up and goes to the kitchen, where her mom and Ian are drinking fresh lemonade. They smile at her, and she smiles back.

"So, Ian," Janelle says. "I guess you were busy making calls today?"

Looking guilty and satisfied at the same time, he says, "Mom helped. She found the phone numbers."

Janelle looks at them both and says, "Thanks for what you did. I guess it worked. I decided I'm trying out again—and I'm determined to make it *and* keep dancing."

"I love the way you're being so positive, honey," her mom says, kissing her cheek. "It really *can* make all the difference."

A NOTE TO GROWN-UPS

Ongoing research by Search Institute, a nonprofit organization based in Minneapolis, Minnesota, shows that young people who succeed have specific assets in their lives—**Developmental Assets** including family support, a caring neighborhood, integrity, resistance skills, self-esteem, and a sense of purpose. This book, along with the other seven books in the **Adding Assets Series for Kids**, empowers young people ages 8–12 to build their own Developmental Assets.

But it's very important to acknowledge that building assets for and with young people is primarily an *adult* responsibility. What kids need most in their lives are grown-ups—parents and other relatives, teachers, school administrators, neighbors, youth leaders, religious leaders, community members, policy makers, advocates, and more—who care about them as individuals. They need adults who care enough to learn their names, to show interest in their lives, to listen when they talk, to provide them with opportunities to realize their potential, to teach them well, to give them sound advice, to serve as good examples, to guide them, to inspire them, to support them when they stumble, and to shield them from harm—as much as is humanly possible these days.

This book focuses on four of the 40 Developmental Assets identified by Search Institute. These are **Internal Assets**—values, skills, and self-perceptions that kids develop *internally,* with your help. The internal assets described here are called the **Positive Identity Assets.** Young people need to believe in their own self-worth, to feel that they have some control over things that happen to them, and to have a sense of purpose in life. The Positive Identity assets work together to help kids form and sustain a bright, optimistic view of their future.

Parents and other adults at home have so much influence over how kids feel about themselves. How we respond to their successes and failures, choices and mistakes can make all the difference. When we love our children, they learn to love themselves. When we criticize them in negative or unconstructive ways, they may learn that they can never please us. Think of yourself as a mirror: What are you reflecting back to your child? What do your words and actions say about him or her? Do you focus on the positive and look for the best in your child? Do you believe in your child's worth and promise? You are key to helping your child develop a set of personal attitudes that will enable him or her to function as an independent, competent, complete person in the world.

A list of all 40 Developmental Assets for middle childhood, with definitions, follows. If you want to know more about the assets, some of the resources listed on pages 84–85 will help you. Or you can visit the Search Institute Web site at *www.search-institute.org.*

Thank you for caring enough about kids to make this book available to the young person or persons in your life. We'd love to hear your success stories, and we welcome your suggestions for adding assets to kids' lives—or improving future editions of this book.

Pamela Espeland and Elizabeth Verdick
Free Spirit Publishing Inc.
217 Fifth Avenue North, Suite 200
Minneapolis, MN 55401-1299
help4kids@freespirit.com

The 40 Developmental Assets for Middle Childhood

EXTERNAL ASSETS

SUPPORT

1. **Family support**—Family life provides high levels of love and support.
2. **Positive family communication**—Parent(s) and child communicate positively. Child feels comfortable seeking advice and counsel from parent(s).
3. **Other adult relationships**—Child receives support from adults other than her or his parent(s).
4. **Caring neighborhood**—Child experiences caring neighbors.
5. **Caring school climate**—Relationships with teachers and peers provide a caring, encouraging school environment.
6. **Parent involvement in schooling**—Parent(s) are actively involved in helping the child succeed in school.

EMPOWERMENT

7. **Community values children**—Child feels valued and appreciated by adults in the community.
8. **Children as resources**—Child is included in decisions at home and in the community.
9. **Service to others**—Child has opportunities to help others in the community.
10. **Safety**—Child feels safe at home, at school, and in her or his neighborhood.

BOUNDARIES AND EXPECTATIONS

11. **Family boundaries**—Family has clear and consistent rules and consequences and monitors the child's whereabouts.
12. **School boundaries**—School provides clear rules and consequences.
13. **Neighborhood boundaries**—Neighbors take responsibility for monitoring the child's behavior.
14. **Adult role models**—Parent(s) and other adults in the child's family, as well as nonfamily adults, model positive, responsible behavior.
15. **Positive peer influence**—Child's closest friends model positive, responsible behavior.
16. **High expectations**—Parent(s) and teachers expect the child to do her or his best at school and in other activities.

CONSTRUCTIVE USE OF TIME

17. **Creative activities**—Child participates in music, art, drama, or creative writing two or more times per week.
18. **Child programs**—Child participates two or more times per week in cocurricular school activities or structured community programs for children.
19. **Religious community**—Child attends religious programs or services one or more times per week.
20. **Time at home**—Child spends some time most days both in high-quality interaction with parent(s) and doing things at home other than watching TV or playing video games.

INTERNAL ASSETS

COMMITMENT TO LEARNING

21. **Achievement motivation**—Child is motivated and strives to do well in school.
22. **Learning engagement**—Child is responsive, attentive, and actively engaged in learning at school and enjoys participating in learning activities outside of school.
23. **Homework**—Child usually hands in homework on time.
24. **Bonding to adults at school**—Child cares about teachers and other adults at school.
25. **Reading for pleasure**—Child enjoys and engages in reading for fun most days of the week.

POSITIVE VALUES

26. **Caring**—Parent(s) tell the child it is important to help other people.
27. **Equality and social justice**—Parent(s) tell the child it is important to speak up for equal rights for all people.
28. **Integrity**—Parent(s) tell the child it is important to stand up for one's beliefs.
29. **Honesty**—Parent(s) tell the child it is important to tell the truth.
30. **Responsibility**—Parent(s) tell the child it is important to accept personal responsibility for behavior.
31. **Healthy lifestyle**—Parent(s) tell the child it is important to have good health habits and an understanding of healthy sexuality.

SOCIAL COMPETENCIES

32. **Planning and decision making**—Child thinks about decisions and is usually happy with the results of her or his decisions.
33. **Interpersonal competence**—Child cares about and is affected by other people's feelings, enjoys making friends, and, when frustrated or angry, tries to calm herself or himself.
34. **Cultural competence**—Child knows and is comfortable with people of different racial, ethnic, and cultural backgrounds and with her or his own cultural identity.
35. **Resistance skills**—Child can stay away from people who are likely to get her or him in trouble and is able to say no to doing wrong or dangerous things.
36. **Peaceful conflict resolution**—Child attempts to resolve conflict nonviolently.

POSITIVE IDENTITY

37. **Personal power**—Child feels he or she has some influence over things that happen in her or his life.
38. **Self-esteem**—Child likes and is proud to be the person he or she is.
39. **Sense of purpose**—Child sometimes thinks about what life means and whether there is a purpose for her or his life.
40. **Positive view of personal future**—Child is optimistic about her or his personal future.

Helpful Resources

Books

Reaching Your Goals by Robin Landew Silverman (New York: Franklin Watts, 2004). To turn a wish into a goal takes creative thinking and organized planning skills. This book shows how to make a plan and see it through to the end.

Stick Up for Yourself! Every Kid's Guide to Personal Power and Positive Self-Esteem by Gershen Kaufman, Ph.D., Lev Raphael, Ph.D., and Pamela Espeland (Minneapolis: Free Spirit Publishing, 1999). It's not always easy to say what's on your mind. With a focus on thinking positively and communicating emotions, this book includes tips and exercises to build confidence and make good choices.

Think for Yourself: A Kid's Guide to Solving Life's Dilemmas and Other Sticky Problems by Cynthia MacGregor (Toronto: Lobster Press, 2003). This book breaks down daily problems into categories: friends, family, grown-ups, and everyday situations. Real-life examples and choices for solutions help you learn to think things through and make good decisions.

What to Do When You're Scared & Worried by James J. Crist (Minneapolis: Free Spirit Publishing, 2004). If you're feeling scared and worried, this book can help you understand and confront troubling feelings. It offers advice and tips for how you can recognize and manage your fears, and how to get help for the hard-to-handle problems that are too big to deal with on your own.

Web sites

Too Smart to Start
www.toosmarttostart.samhsa.gov/youth.html
Are you smart enough NOT to start using alcohol or other drugs? Read advice from teens about how and why to say no. Do crossword puzzles and word searches. Tell your parents or other family adults about this Web site; there's good stuff here for grown-ups, too.

Youth Service America
www.servenet.org
Connect to organizations and service projects in your area. Type in your ZIP code, skills, and interests to find the best experience for you.

Youth Venture
www.youthventure.org
Youth Venture believes every young person can make a difference. Do you have a solution to a problem in your community? Youth Venture invests in the ideas of young people who create, launch, and lead organizations, clubs, or businesses that provide a positive, lasting benefit in a school, neighborhood, or large community.

FOR ADULTS

Books

Building Assets Is Elementary: Group Activities for Helping Kids Ages 8–12 Succeed by Search Institute (Minneapolis: Search Institute, 2004). Promoting creativity, time-management skills, kindness, manners, and more, this flexible activity book includes over 50 easy-to-use group exercises for the classroom or youth group.

Parents Do Make a Difference: How to Raise Kids with Solid Character, Strong Minds, and Caring Hearts by Michele Borba (New York: Jossey-Bass, 1999). Based on nationwide research and pilot programs in elementary schools, this book combines simple steps to reinforce positive self-esteem in kids.

The Power of Positive Talk: Words to Help Every Child Succeed by Douglas Bloch, M.A., with Jon Merritt, M.S. (Minneapolis: Free Spirit Publishing, 2003). Affirmations can heal hurts, build self-esteem, and empower us to face life with confidence and courage. This book helps kids and adults learn affirmations for many situations and challenges.

What Kids Need to Succeed: Proven, Practical Ways to Raise Good Kids by Peter L. Benson, Ph.D., Judy Galbraith, M.A., and Pamela Espeland (Minneapolis: Free Spirit Publishing, 1994). More than 900 specific, concrete suggestions help adults help children build Developmental Assets at home, at school, and in the community.

What Young Children Need to Succeed: Working Together to Build Assets from Birth to Age 11 by Jolene L. Roehlkepartain and Nancy Leffert, Ph.D. (Minneapolis: Free Spirit Publishing, 2000). Hundreds of practical, concrete ideas help adults build Developmental Assets for children in four different age groups: birth to 12 months, ages 1–2, 3–5, and 6–11. Includes inspiring true stories from across the United States.

Web sites

Connect for Kids
www.connectforkids.org

Tips, articles, resources, volunteer opportunities, and more for adults who want to improve the lives of children in their community and beyond. Includes the complete text of Richard Louv's book *101 Things You Can Do for Our Children's Future*.

Search Institute
www.search-institute.org

Through dynamic research and analysis, this independent nonprofit organization works to promote healthy, active, and content youth and communities.

Index

About the Authors

Both Pamela Espeland and Elizabeth Verdick have written many books for children and teens.

Pamela is the coauthor (with Peter L. Benson and Judy Galbraith) of *What Kids Need to Succeed* and *What Teens Need to Succeed* and the author of *Succeed Every Day*, all based on Search Institute's concept of the 40 Developmental Assets. She is the author of *Life Lists for Teens* and the coauthor (with Gershen Kaufman and Lev Raphael) of *Stick Up for Yourself!*

Elizabeth is a children's book writer and editor. She is the author of *Germs Are Not for Sharing, Tails Are Not for Pulling, Teeth Are Not for Biting, Words Are Not for Hurting,* and *Feet Are Not for Kicking,* and coauthor (with Marjorie Lisovskis) of *How to Take the GRRRR Out of Anger* and (with Trevor Romain) of *Stress Can Really Get on Your Nerves!* and *True or False? Tests Stink!*

Pamela and Elizabeth first worked together on *Making Every Day Count.* They live in Minnesota with their families and pets.

More Titles in the Adding Assets Series for Kids

Each book is 80–100 pages, softcover, two-color illustrations, 5⅛" x 7", $9.95. For ages 8–12.
To order, call **1.800.735.7323** or visit *www.freespirit.com*

People Who Care About You
Kids build the six Support Assets: Family Support, Positive Family Communication, Other Adult Relationships, Caring Neighborhood, Caring School Climate, and Parent Involvement in Schooling.

Helping Out and Staying Safe
Kids build the four Empowerment Assets: Community Values Children, Children as Resources, Service to Others, and Safety.

Doing and Being Your Best
Kids build the six Boundaries and Expectations Assets: Family Boundaries, School Boundaries, Neighborhood Boundaries, Adult Role Models, Positive Peer Influence, and High Expectations.

Smart Ways to Spend Your Time
Kids build the four Constructive Use of Time Assets: Creative Activities, Child Programs, Religious Community, and Time at Home.

Loving to Learn
Kids build the five Commitment to Learning Assets: Achievement Motivation, Learning Engagement, Homework, Bonding to Adults at School, and Reading for Pleasure.

Knowing and Doing What's Right
Kids build the six Positive Values Assets: Caring, Equality and Social Justice, Integrity, Honesty, Responsibility, and Healthy Lifestyle.

Making Choices and Making Friends
Kids build the five Social Competencies Assets: Planning and Decision Making, Interpersonal Competence, Cultural Competence, Resistance Skills, and Peaceful Conflict Resolution.

A Leader's Guide to The Adding Assets Series for Kids

A comprehensive, easy-to-use curriculum for building all 40 Developmental Assets, with activities, discussion prompts, handouts for parents and other family adults, and a scope-and-sequence for standards-based education. The included CD-ROM features all of the reproducible forms from the book and an additional 40 pages of student handouts used in the sessions. For grades 3–6.

$39.95; 288 pp.; softcover; lay-flat binding; 8½" x 11".

Fast, Friendly, and Easy to Use
www.freespirit.com

Browse the catalog

Info & extras

Many ways to search

Quick check-out

Stop in and see!

To place an order or to request a free catalog of SELF-HELP FOR KIDS® and SELF-HELP FOR TEENS® materials, please write, call, email, or visit our Web site:

Free Spirit Publishing Inc.
217 Fifth Avenue North • Suite 200 • Minneapolis, MN 55401-1299
toll-free 800.735.7323 • local 612.338.2068 • fax 612.337.5050
help4kids@freespirit.com • www.freespirit.com

Dodgeville Public Library
139 S. Iowa St.
Dodgeville, WI 53533